TOOLS FOR CAREGIVERS

- **F&P LEVEL:** C
- **WORD COUNT:** 55
- **CURRICULUM CONNECTIONS:** opposites

Skills to Teach

- **HIGH-FREQUENCY WORDS:** her, his, is, one, the, this
- **CONTENT WORDS:** big, clean, cold, dark, day, dirty, dry, empty, full, glass, good, hair, hot, light, night, plane, sand, shirt, short, small, tall, water, wet
- **PUNCTUATION:** exclamation point, periods
- **WORD STUDY:** long /a/, spelled *ai* (*hair*); long /a/, spelled *ay* (*day*); long /e/, spelled *ea* (*clean*); long /e/, spelled *y* (*dirty, empty*); long /i/, spelled *i* (*dry*)
- **TEXT TYPE:** factual description

Before Reading Activities

- Read the title and give a simple statement of the main idea.
- Have students "walk" through the book and talk about what they see in the pictures.
- Introduce new vocabulary by having students predict the first letter and locate the word in the text.
- Discuss any unfamiliar concepts that are in the text.

After Reading Activities

On the board, make a list of the opposites featured in the book. Have a column for each. What else can readers compare as opposites? What is something that can be wet or dry? What is something in the room that can be big or small? Write the opposites across from each other on the board. What other opposites can readers identify?

Tadpole Books are published by Jump!, 5357 Penn Avenue South, Minneapolis, MN 55419, www.jumplibrary.com

Copyright ©2021 Jump. International copyright reserved in all countries. No part of this book may be reproduced in any form without written permission from the publisher.

Editor: Jenna Gleisner   **Designer:** Anna Peterson

Photo Credits: ventdusud/Shutterstock, cover (left); Rawpixel.com/Shutterstock, cover (right); Alexia Khruscheva/Shutterstock, 1; Cultura Creative/Alamy, 3; aapsky/Shutterstock, 4–5 (background); yesstock/Shutterstock, 4–5 (foreground); S_Photo/Shutterstock, 6; ARTEM VOROPAI/Shutterstock, 7; Sunny studio/Shutterstock, 2tr, 2br, 8, 9; Serhiy Kobyakov/Shutterstock, 2mr, 10; exopixel/Shutterstock, 2ml, 11; StockImageFactory.com/Shutterstock, 12–13; Choreograph/iStock, 2bl, 14; Yuganov Konstantin/Shutterstock, 2tl, 15; Alexlukin/Shutterstock, 16.

Library of Congress Cataloging-in-Publication Data
Names: Kenan, Tessa, author.
Title: Let's learn opposites / by Tessa Kenan.
Description: Minneapolis: Jump!, Inc., 2021. | Series: Fun first concepts | Includes index.
Identifiers: LCCN 2020023915 (print) | LCCN 2020023916 (ebook) | ISBN 9781645277682 (hardcover)
ISBN 9781645277699 (paperback) | ISBN 9781645277705 (ebook)
Subjects: LCSH: English language—Synonyms and antonyms—Juvenile literature. | Polarity—Juvenile literature.
Classification: LCC PE1591 .K37 2021 (print) | LCC PE1591 (ebook) | DDC 428.1—dc23
LC record available at https://lccn.loc.gov/2020023915
LC ebook record available at https://lccn.loc.gov/2020023916

FUN FIRST CONCEPTS

LET'S LEARN OPPOSITES

by Tessa Kenan

TABLE OF CONTENTS

tadpole
books

WORDS TO KNOW

dark

dry

empty

full

light

wet

OPPOSITES

One is tall.
One is short.

plane

This plane is big.

This plane is small.

sand

The sand is hot.

water

The water is cold.

Her hair is wet.

hair

Her hair is dry.

glass

This glass is full.

This glass is empty.

Her shirt is dirty.

His shirt is clean.

Day is light.

Night is dark.
Good night!

LET'S REVIEW!

Point to the glass that is full. Point to the glass that is empty.

INDEX